Mary Colson

WAYLAND

Published in paperback in 2014 by Wayland
Copyright © Wayland 2014

Wayland
338 Euston Road
London NW1 3BH

Wayland Australia
Level 17/207 Kent Street
Sydney, NSW 2000

Produced for Wayland by Calcium
Design concept by Lisa Peacock

Picture acknowledgements
Carbonfund.org: 33t; Dreamstime: 13, 86ccyy 22, Americanspirit 28b, Piero Cruciatti 23t, Hou Guima 27t, Himiko2023909 34b, Hsc 31, 38, Huating 25b, 26, Logit 2, 7tr, 17t, 17b, 24, Pavel Losevsky 34t, Hugo Maes 23b, Bartlomiej Magierowski 20, Pumba1 43t, Huguette Roe 30, Springdt313 39, Thisisdon 27m, Lukasz Tymszan 37, Zhanglianxun 25t; Shutterstock: 06photo 42, anaken2012 32t, Guryanov Andrey 8t, Yuri Arcurs 8b, Darren Baker 5b, beboy 33m, Dmitry Berkut 40, Ajay Bhaskar 7b, C Jimenez 18t, dotshock 43b, Barone Firenze 44, Fotocrisis 6b, 10, hacohob 29, Pablo Hidalgo 11b, hxdbzxy 15t, Jan S. 12, Konstantin L 7t, lightpoet 45, Alberto Loyo 36, Bartlomiej Magierowski 15b, Oleksiy Mark 21, mikeledray 33b, Monkey Business Images 4, paintings 41, pio3 9, Pressmaster 5t, Huguette Roe 28t, soulgems 14, George Spade 7tl, 11t, Vlasov Volodymyr 18b, Vydrin 16, wavebreakmedia 19, 35, Feng Yu 32b.

A catalogue record for this book is available from the British Library.

ISBN: 978 0 7502 8331 1
Printed in China
10 9 8 7 6 5 4 3 2 1

Wayland is a division of Hachette Children's Books,
an Hachette UK company.
www.hachette.co.uk

CONTENTS

PURCHASING POWER

When you shop for a cool new phone, do you think about how your purchase might affect people elsewhere in the world? Do you ever wonder where your must-have games console comes from? Would you buy your shiny new computer if you knew the keypad was made by child workers in China?

SHOP TO CHANGE THE WORLD

The gadgets you buy and the money you spend affect people elsewhere. There's a vast global network or **supply chain** to ensure that the products you want arrive on the shop shelves.

World wide web

The IT and electronics industry is a global giant - the fastest growing business on the planet. All over the **developed world**, there is high **consumer** demand for computers, mobile phones and electronic games. In order to feed this greed for gadgets, there is a human and an environmental cost.

The **UN** estimates that we replace our phones every 18 months and that only 0.5% of them are recycled. The rest go to **landfill**. Along with unwanted games consoles, old computer towers and broken monitors, they leak poisonous lead and mercury into the **water courses**.

Today, techno-gadgets are central to many people's lives. How important are they to yours?

Going overseas

Many large western companies get their products made overseas where people's wages are low. This means the company makes more profit. If the products were made in a country such as the USA where wages are higher, the company would make much less profit.

Most offices today function with electronic equipment, such as computers, printers and telephones.

Factory conditions

Many technology factories are in countries and parts of the world where the laws are very different, such as China, Central America and Asia. The workers live and work long hours in poor conditions and receive very little pay. Factories like these are called **sweatshops**.

People power

Computers, mobiles and games consoles look very clean and shiny but is that the whole picture? This book looks at the links between the technology we buy and use in our daily lives and where it comes from. It will examine the links between supply, demand, labour conditions, resources and waste. It will also look at **ethical shopping** and how things are improving. It will explain that you can shop to change the world.

SUPPLY AND DEMAND

China is the world's largest producer of electronic items. Over 1.3 million people work in Chinese 'computer cities' where all the factories make products for western companies.

Family and leisure time is often spent playing computer and video games together.

TECHNO-WORLD MAP

• Over 75% of American homes have a computer.

• Sweden is the most technologically advanced country on Earth. Most people have access to broadband and mobile phone reception and live technology-based lives.

• The USA uses more energy per person per year than any other country on the planet.

• Around 77% of households in Britain have Internet access.

• Niger in Africa has the least amount of computers per household in the world. Less than 1 in a 1,000 homes has a PC.

• Silver and tin are mined in Peru and Mexico.

• Tantalum is mined in the Democratic Republic of Congo.

• Copper is mined in Chile.

• Platinum for a hard drive comes from South Africa.

• There are more computers per household in Sweden than anywhere else in the world.

• Beryllium is mined in Kazakhstan. This is used to insulate microprocessors.

• 'Made in China' means that all the various parts were probably made elsewhere but put together in Chinese factories.

• South Korea is the first country on Earth to have all of its citizens on a wi-fi network.

• Bangalore is known as the Silicon Valley of India because it is an IT city.

• Circuit boards are assembled in the Philippines and Malaysia.

• Gold is mined in Australia.

CHAPTER 1

WORLD WIDE WEB

When you buy a product in a shop and take it home, it is the end of a long chain. Your computer, mobile or games console began life a long time before you owned it. This chapter will look at the supply chain of technology products, from the resources used to make the products, to the factory conditions of the assembly line and the journey to your door.

Young people are technology experts and want the latest products.

Supply chain

The supply chain is the process of how a product is sourced, made, transported to a shop and then to your home. The plastic used to make your console might come from the oil fields of the Persian Gulf. The silicon chip inside your computer might come from the USA, the screen may be produced in Japan and the whole thing might be assembled in a factory in China. The product will then be packaged with cardboard perhaps made in Canada, shipped, and some months later, it might be finally bought by you.

Modern computer stores are high-tech in design as well as in the products they sell.

Being informed

It's easy to be a super consumer. Before you buy, you could do an online search about the product and the company. This will tell you their track record with regard to working conditions at their factories, how they treat their workers and whether they are concerned about the environment. You can also write or email the company and ask them about how they make their technology products. Having this information can help you to make decisions about your purchases.

SHOP TO CHANGE THE WORLD

When you buy things in a shop, you are called a consumer. You decide and choose what you consume. The labels on the box will tell you where a product is made. It will also give you information about who made it and whether the product uses recycled materials or is eco-friendly. The best labels will also tell you how to safely dispose of or recycle the item once you've finished with it. (See page 47 for details of electronics recycling.)

RAW MATERIALS

More than 130 million computers are produced every year across the world. With these huge numbers comes an enormous need for raw materials and energy. To make a computer and a screen takes around 240 kg of **fossil fuels**, 21 kg of chemicals and over 1,300 kg of water. This is more than the weight of a car of resources for each computer.

Computer construction

Have you ever thought about what you need to make a computer? To begin with, you need plastic for the keyboard, glass for the screen and metal for the key springs, but what else do you need?

Some technology products need over 1,000 different materials to make them. This means extracting resources from the ground and processing them, resulting in a high environmental cost.

Extracting copper from this mine in Chile creates sulphuric acid as a waste product. This is toxic to humans, wildlife and water sources.

Recipe for a computer

You won't have room in your shopping basket for everything so just get the basics. Most are available from all good oil fields, industrial mines, processing plants and chemical factories.

Large scale oil drilling feeds the technology industry's need for resources.

Material	Computer use?	Eco-impact?
Plastic	Computer casing, keyboard and keys	High energy use to extract oil
Silicon	Screen, computer chip	Poisonous carbon monoxide is created during the extraction process
Copper	Wires, computer chip and circuit board	Waste products become toxic to the environment; high water and energy use
Platinum	Hard drive	Very high energy use to extract; water pollution and toxic waste
Lead	Screen	Air pollution, toxic waste
Tin	USB ports	Destruction of forests and coral reefs in some tin-mining nations
Aluminium	To absorb heat and keep computer cool	Extraction process creates carbon dioxide, which is toxic in large amounts
Mercury	Switches	Water pollution, highly toxic
Cadmium	Battery	Highly toxic, air pollution
PVC	Casing for computer cables and circuit boards	Poisons the air where it is burned

SUPPLY AND DEMAND

The world's largest copper mine is in the Atacama Desert in South America, the driest place on Earth. Up to 500 gallons of water per second are required to extract copper so large desalination plants purify sea water that is pumped across the desert. Sulphuric acid is a toxic waste product of this process and it needs to be disposed of very carefully.

Silicon and copper are used to make silicon chips such as these, the basic element of all computers.

SWEATSHOPS: HUMAN FACTORIES

Once the resources have been extracted and used to make the parts required, the products must be assembled. This next step in the supply chain is sometimes done by machines but because of the small parts, a lot of the products in the IT and technology industries are assembled by people.

SUPPLY AND DEMAND

It is estimated that 85% of sweatshop workers are between 15 and 25 years old. They work 60–80 hours per week and sometimes receive only pennies for their work. They have to spend 50–75% of their income on food because their wages are so low.

Consumer demand

In the West, while meeting the demand for cheaper products, companies look for ways to cut costs so that their profits stay high. In order to do this they often set up factories overseas where people are paid less. Some of the workers in these factories experience dreadful conditions. These factories, known as sweatshops, are an unfortunate part of the global business chain called supply and demand.

Child labour

The cheapest workers of all are children and some sweatshops employ hundreds of underage labourers. Many of the children must work to help their parents, who are not paid enough to provide for the family. An education is out of the question for these children, who have to work instead of going to school.

Living standards for sweatshop workers in some countries can be very low. The poorest people live in slums, such as here in Mumbai, India.

A life of labour

The working conditions in sweatshops are often very poor or even unsafe. Workers are forced to work overtime, made to work in dangerous and unhealthy environments, and threatened if they complain. They may also have to handle toxic chemical paints, **solvents** and glues with their bare hands in closed rooms with no fresh air.

Global shame

Sweatshops exist all over the world, from Central and South America to Asia and certain regions of Europe. There are even sweatshops in US cities such as New York, San Francisco and Los Angeles.

SHOP TO CHANGE THE WORLD

Fair trade means paying workers a fair wage for their work. There is a special logo that all fair trade products have on their packaging. Sometimes, they cost a little bit more, but it does mean that they are made in factories where people work in good conditions. It makes the supply chain fairer for everyone.

In this factory in Shenzhen, China, workers make component parts for CCTV cameras.

THE SUPPLY CHAIN

The primary purpose of any business is to make money. The technology industry is so international and competitive that businesses will do their best to keep on top. This flow chart explains how the raw materials, factories and workers can all play their part in keeping **manufacturing costs** down and maximising profit.

1. A technology company in a developed country, such as the USA, wants to make computers, mobile phones and games consoles. There's lots of competition from other companies, and consumers want cheap goods so...

2. ...they gather the raw materials required from dozens of different sources and companies all over the world. They drive a hard bargain and get the materials as cheaply as possible.

Modern office buildings can often hide the grim realities of the supply chain.

7. The American company pays a different company to manage the factory operations and to make the products.

8. The workers live and work at the factories. They assemble techno-gadgets for less than a dollar an hour and work up to 80 hours per week. They can get fired without any notice and rarely have a day off.

9. The technology company owners probably never see the factory so they can turn a blind eye to working conditions.

In the Far East, there are many overcrowded cities with large numbers of people looking for jobs.

3. American labour costs are too high so the company uses factories overseas in developing countries, such as China, Taiwan or the Philippines, where wages are much lower. This is called **outsourcing**.

4. The governments of these developing countries are pleased to have American money being invested and to have lots of jobs being created.

6. The employment agency gives unemployed people work in the factories for a fee. The workers then spend months paying this off before they make any money themselves.

5. The technology company employs another company or employment agency to hire workers.

10. The finished product is packaged, shipped and sold all over the world with as little cost and as much profit as possible.

Workers on an assembly line spend many hours at their workstation.

End of the line?

Whether it's a cherished smartphone, tablet computer or games console, the technology was probably made and assembled in Asia by workers who have few rights and often toil under sweatshop-like conditions. Who do you think is responsible for keeping things like this and what can be done to change the situation?

REPLACING PEOPLE?

When you think of a high-tech factory, what do you picture? Do you see people in white overalls operating space-age machinery in clean white rooms? Or do you see row upon row of low-paid workers picking computer chips off a conveyor belt in a dark and dingy warehouse? Whatever you imagine, you've probably only got part of the picture.

Robot world

Many technology companies are taking the step from a human workforce to a robot one. Some companies who have been found to use sweatshop labour have invested in robots. The company can maximise their profits without forcing people to work in bad conditions. Do you think this is a step in the right direction? Is this the answer to poor factory conditions? What about people's jobs?

Is this a vision of the future? Could all technology factories replace people with robots?

In this factory in China, workers are given protective clothing and face masks so they don't inhale chemicals.

Uniting for change

Not every company is going super-high-tech and workers in some factories are getting together to campaign for change. By protesting and going on strike, the workers hope to raise awareness of their harsh working conditions. They are starting to stand up for their **human rights**. They want their bosses to make positive changes, not simply to replace them with robots.

What's a union?

A union is a special group that represents people's opinions or their professional interests. It might be a group of teachers or nurses or factory workers who are seeking improvements at work or in their pay. Having a few key people to speak up on behalf of many is an effective way to get issues and feelings raised. Union leaders meet with bosses and sometimes government officials and can make change happen.

CONSUMER NATION

What are the pros and cons of using robots instead of workers?

Pros
1. Robots don't need paying
2. They won't go on strike
3. They can work all day long, without needing a break

Cons
1. Millions of people become unemployed
2. 'Computer cities' turn into ghost towns with mass **poverty**
3. The human sweatshop problem simply moves to a place where wages are even lower

CHAPTER 2

WORKING PEOPLE

Think about what you use a computer and your phone for. Games? Email? Contacting friends? Now, think about what your parents use them for. It's likely that they rely on them for quite a lot of their daily lives, from ordering groceries and finding out what's on in the area, to checking their bank account. These gadgets are amazing and we would find it hard to live without them, but there is a cost to our technology. This chapter looks at the different people, often many thousands of miles away, who are paying the price.

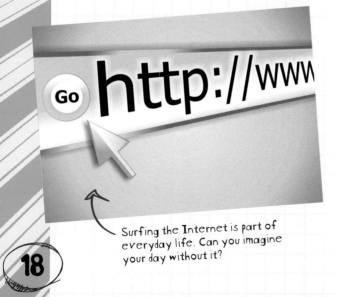

Surfing the Internet is part of everyday life. Can you imagine your day without it?

Working life

You've probably heard your mum or dad come home and moan about work sometimes. Maybe they're tired or they've had a bad or busy day. This happens to everybody sometimes, but not every day. The electronics industry is one of the worst businesses for ensuring good quality work spaces for its employees, particularly during manufacture and assembly.

Research and development

When a business develops a new product such as a tablet computer or a smartphone, it takes many years of work to perfect it. There's a lot of trial and error and sometimes a company will spend millions of pounds before abandoning the project altogether. Even for the successful products, there is a massive investment of time and money before it ever gets to the shops, so businesses try to get back some of that money in the manufacturing and price. It might only cost £50 to make a computer if it's made in, China, for example, where the wages are low. However, we pay a lot more to cover the years of product development.

Many students rely on technology, such as tablets and computers, to access the Internet to research their studies.

SHOP TO CHANGE THE WORLD

It's important to think before you buy, so as you read through this chapter, ask yourself the following questions:
1. Should more money be spent on the workers?
2. If it was, would that improve conditions?
3. Is more money always the answer?
4. What could businesses do to change things?
5. What could you and your family do to change things?
Talk about your answers with your mum or dad and think about who you think is responsible for how things are. How could you help to change things?

CASE STUDY 1
COMPUTER CHILDREN

Children all over the world enjoy playing on their computers, phones and games consoles. It can help their social skills and their coordination, and it's a part of modern childhood. But there are some computer children who never get to play with any of the gadgets we now take for granted: they are the forgotten workers in the technology chain.

Overworked, underpaid and overlooked

China. A factory where products are made for a Western technology company. There are wooden benches either side of a slow-moving conveyor belt which is carrying webcams. The benches are full of workers. Some of the workers look very young. Chen is 14 years old.

Like all the child workers, Chen has to stand up during his shifts which can last up to 15 hours. He can also be told to work overtime on top of this. His wages are so low that he earns less than a dollar an hour.

Like this child worker, not all children enjoy the freedom to have a childhood.

CCD VIDEO CAMERA

SUPPLY AND DEMAND

The top ten global technology companies are worth hundreds of billions of pounds. Many of their workers are in China and India where the wages are low and rules are sometimes overlooked. Can child workers be protected? Yes, if western companies and host governments demand a better deal for everyone.

There is a vast wealth gap between a technology company's head-office executives and the workers making its products in factories.

Feeding the family

Chen's parents work at a nearby factory, but they hardly ever see each other. Chen sends his earnings home to his grandparents. This helps to feed his younger brothers and sisters. They will probably have to start work when they're 14, too.

Lost childhood

Chen misses out on many things, but mostly he's missed out on a childhood. Chen hasn't gone to school and he doesn't have free time. Because his parents aren't there, he has no one to talk to about his problems. He misses his parents but he has to work to help the family.

Child protection

The International Labour Organisation (ILO) has made June 12th the World Day Against Child Labour. This day helps to raise awareness of the suffering of child workers like Chen around the world. The ILO has a legal code which states that child labour must be **outlawed** and that there must be a minimum age for employment, which it says should not be below the age for finishing compulsory schooling.

WORKING WOMEN'S RIGHTS

Millions of workers, most of them women, work in tens of thousands of sweatshops around the world. Campaigning organisations estimate that 85% of sweatshop workers are young women between the ages of 15-25.

Many of the workers in Chinese technology factories are women. They often go to work in order to pay for a better education for their children. But this comes at a high price for both their health and their family life.

Wage slaves

The wages that most women are paid in sweatshops won't give them a basic standard of living. Young women are often drawn into work by employment agents promising them good pay abroad. The women pay the agents who give them contracts to sign. The contracts say that the women workers have to pay money each month to the agents. They can be paying for years as there are no controls over the dishonest agents.

A female factory worker in China may not have as many rights as female workers in other parts of the world.

Harsh choice

Some women in Central American and Mexican factories live in fear of being fired if they become pregnant. There is little chance of finding another job as a pregnant woman and there is no **maternity pay**. Many female workers put up with awful conditions without complaining. Unions are banned in many countries so the workers don't even have the chance to air their views.

In some factories, like this one in China, the equipment is often old and the workstations badly lit.

Changing times?

The UN and human rights organisations such as Amnesty International, are working to improve conditions for women in employment around the world. If you want to get involved, check out the anti-slavery campaigns on their websites.

Some factories provide better conditions, but the wages may still be very low.

CONSUMER NATION

Do you think it's a good idea to employ women in developing countries?

Pros

1. By allowing women to earn their own money, they are more in control of their lives and not reliant on others.
2. Both parents should contribute to a family's income, not just the father.
3. The more skilled the whole workforce is, the better it is for a country.

Cons

1. If women work, they are unable to be a full-time mother.
2. If workers become pregnant, employers may think it's a waste of their job training.
3. Children need at least one parent at home to be a role model.

CASE STUDY 2

EAT, WORK, SLEEP: LIFE IN A SWEATSHOP COMPOUND

Imagine a job advert that promises food and accommodation on top of your pay. Sounds good, doesn't it? Yet, things aren't always what they seem.

Computer factory, Zhongguancun, Beijing, China

It's 7pm. Bai has already sat on his hard wooden stool in his place in the assembly line for nearly 12 hours. It's Sunday. He hasn't had a day off for over three weeks. His eyes are starting to close with tiredness and he rubs them to keep awake. *Click*. Yawning, he picks up another keyboard key and clicks it into place. *Click*. He knows the QWERTY keyboard off by heart now. *Click*. He can't read or speak English and he's never used a computer, but he knows the QWERTY keyboard off by heart. *Click*.

Every second counts

Around 500 computer keyboards an hour move down the assembly line, one every 7.2 seconds. Like his co-workers, Bai has just 1.1 seconds to snap and click each key into place. He will repeat this action 3,250 times every hour. That's 35,750 times a day, 250,250 times a week and over one million times a month.

Workers on an assembly line in a factory producing laptop computers in China. Assembly line work is extremely repetitive and pressurised.

All Bai thinks is that every hour, he's earned another 60 cents to send home to help feed his family. *Click*. He reaches for another keyboard key. *Click*. He needs the toilet but he knows he's not allowed to go during shifts. *Click*.

Far-away family

Bai is just one of over two thousand workers in this factory. He's been on keyboards since he arrived in the city from the countryside six months ago. His home town and family are over 200 km away. He hasn't been back once. He's had two days off each month since he arrived, but he had to spend most of those days queuing to make a ten-minute phone call home. He's hoping to travel home for three days at the end of the year.

Factory workers on assembly lines work at high speed for hours.

The better factory compounds have leisure facilities for the workers to use when they're not on their shift.

Day's end

Bai's shift comes to an end. With a final click of the final keyboard key in place, he stands and stretches. Before he has walked ten paces towards the door, another worker has taken his place. The factory never stops.

After some noodle soup in the canteen, Bai returns to his dormitory. Twelve workers share a room. They wash with hot water from a bucket. Bai sits on his narrow metal bed. His whole body aches with tiredness. He lies down and reaches for the light switch. *Click*.

MIGRANT WORKERS

Guangdong Province, China. A vast region of farmland, remote villages and small close-knit communities. The crops have failed again and there's no work. Many of the young men and women from the village will have to leave to go and find work in the cities.

Many kilometres away, the city welcomes new arrivals from the countryside every day. Hundreds arrive each week. Carrying their bags of belongings, they search for a job. They don't know when they'll see their families again, but it's their only chance to make a living. This is the grim reality facing tens of thousands of **migrant workers** in China.

Dream job?

The technology industry thrives in the cities of Guangdong Province. Signs on factories boast of good working conditions and decent pay. But once inside, the workers are put to use straight away on assembly lines. It's not such a dream job after all.

SUPPLY AND DEMAND

The majority of the workers in computer factories are young, single, migrant workers aged between 16 and 25 years old. Their official papers show that they are registered as country people. This means that they can be sacked and sent back as soon as the demand for products goes down. No matter how long they have been working in the city, they are not permitted to stay there permanently.

Company buses pick workers up to take them to a factory in Zhuhai, China.

This chemical factory in Beijing bellows polluting smoke out into the city's skyline. It is a similar sight in many cities throughout China.

Desperate people leave their homes and journey to cities, such as Guangzhou, looking for work. Those who don't find a job may end up begging on the streets.

No protection

If the workers want to get married, the factory owners reduce their pay rather than give them annual leave. If a female worker has a child, the schooling of that child is the responsibility of the worker's home community as far as the owners are concerned. If the worker has an accident and suffers a serious injury, there is no cash support from the factory owners. The injured worker has to return to their home village to be looked after. There is no sick pay or **disability benefit** from the government.

Who's to blame?

What do you think? Is it the fault of the factory owners? Or should western technology companies check factory conditions more? What about us? Should we change our buying habits?

CHAPTER 3

WASTE MATTERS

When your PC or mobile has started to go slow or you want to upgrade to the latest model, what do you do with it? Where does it go? The technology we use to manage our lives fuels a need for more power and that has consequences, too. This chapter looks at the issues surrounding electronic waste, along with its impact on the environment and human health.

Sorting through technology waste can be dangerous for workers if they don't wear protective clothing.

Poison power?

Mobile phones, laptops and games console remote controls are all run on different kinds of batteries. Batteries contain at least eight toxic metals, including cadmium, lead, zinc, manganese, nickel, mercury, silver and lithium. They also contain acids. Whilst they are being used, they are safe. The problems come once they're finished with. If batteries are thrown away into a normal landfill site, they can start to leak their toxic chemicals into the groundwater. Mercury batteries are gradually being phased out, but all the metals contained in batteries are harmful to humans if they get into our food chain.

High energy use

All our gadgets are energy-greedy. Whether they are plugged into the mains or use batteries, gadgets keep up a constant demand for power.

The more electricity we require, the more needs to be produced. In the UK, most electricity comes from coal-fired power stations which pollute the air with carbon dioxide, and nuclear power stations which create toxic waste that has to be stored extremely carefully.

An average computer uses 200 watts per hour. Over a year, this is 584,000 watts of energy that must be sourced. This is around four times the amount of energy a lightbulb uses and would power over 500 toasters.

Electric equality?

On average, a UK household uses 4,800 kilowatts of electricity per year with nearly one-third used to power techno products. The USA has the highest energy use of anywhere in the world. Developing countries such as India and China are catching up fast, and are using almost as much electricity. This isn't sustainable for the planet.

SUPPLY AND DEMAND

The more our lives depend on technology, the more energy we need to power them. Did you know that we use most energy when we leave our electronic gadgets on standby? Leaving appliances on standby rather than turning them off makes up 5 to 10% of household energy use. That's about £86 per family in the UK, or £1.3 billion nationwide.

DESIGNED TO DUMP?

Electronic waste is the fastest growing sector of household and business waste and it all needs to go somewhere. Many local councils have recycling centres where electronic goods can be taken and then processed, but what does 'processed' mean? And are manufacturers doing anything to make all our techno-gadgets less throwaway?

Enormous amounts of e-waste

E-waste is the fastest growing part of our rubbish. More than 1 million tonnes a year needs to be dealt with. It's estimated that around 40% of the heavy metals found in UK landfills, including lead, mercury and cadmium, comes from electronic equipment throwouts. Global e-waste is more than 50 million tonnes and only 10% is recycled.

E-waste mountains are growing fast as we update and replace our techno-gadgets.

The developed world has an unquenchable thirst for circuit boards for new high-tech gadgets.

Hiding the problem

Much of our e-waste, such as old computer monitors, televisions, games consoles and mobile phones, isn't recycled in this country but shipped abroad. E-waste from countries all over Europe is sent to places such as the Far East, India and African countries such as Nigeria and Ghana. European governments pay those nations to store their waste. The problem is the waste isn't sorted properly or made safe first, so much of it is toxic.

Health hazard

When televisions, mobile phones and computer processors are broken down, lead, mercury and other chemicals are released into the air and water sources, causing pollution. In poor countries, workers don't have protective clothing and there are few, if any, health and safety regulations. Once these chemicals get into drinking wells, people can develop serious illnesses such as cancer.

SUPPLY AND DEMAND

Did you know that 40–50% of the environmental impact of a mobile phone occurs as its wiring boards and circuits are being made? After purchase, the average user then replaces their mobile phone every 11 to 18 months. The discarded phones then contribute to the e-waste mountain.

SHOP TO CHANGE THE WORLD

Various **pressure groups**, such as Ethical Consumer are campaigning for the industry to change. They want manufacturers to be responsible for removing harmful chemicals from their products and for safely recycling or disposing of their gadgets.

ECO-ELECTRONICS

Some technology firms are starting to sit up and take notice of the environment and the problems that the supply chain creates. Companies such as IBM abide by a code not to use sweatshops and not to pollute. Organisations such as United Pepper source ethical electronics and then sell them online. Bamboo plastic casings for tablet computers and low-energy-use screens are part of a new wave of products on the market.

SHOP TO CHANGE THE WORLD

How can you measure a company in terms of its environmental record, human rights and fair wages? There are many pressure groups and organisations such as Better World Shopper that focus on finding out this important information. They use dozens of different data sources and company reports to arrive at their conclusions and rankings. If a company finds itself ranked in the top ten worst companies, it might be forced to change its bad business practices because it doesn't want poor publicity. (For more details, see page 47.)

The lithium used in PC, camera and phone batteries is highly toxic and so must be disposed of safely.

PCs don't have to go out of date. They can be upgraded rather than replaced.

Eco-labels

Across the world, there are many different labels and logos for products that are more eco-friendly or ethical, to help you when you're shopping. The most international are the 'BEST' logo, which represents low lead use in batteries, and the 'CarbonFree' label, which is on products made with very low **greenhouse gas** emissions. 'Earthsure' and 'Energy Star' are other labels on products that show good environmental awareness, whilst the 'SEE' (what you are buying into) label is on products which avoid sweatshops.

Reuse and recycle!

Top tips for techno-trash!

Many organisations suggest the following ways to recycle or re-use your old gadgets:

1. Donate for reuse if possible.
2. Find a recycler near you.
3. See if the manufacturer has a free recycling programme.
4. Find out which shops in your area will take old PCs.
5. Lots of companies offer money back in exchange for old phones. If you upgrade they can safely dispose of your old one.
6. Recycle rechargeable batteries.
7. Use Freecycle or another community recycling programme.

SAVE THE EARTH
RECYCLE

Remember to recycle your high-tech products and you'll be a super consumer!

CHAPTER 4

TECHNO-ADDICTS

How much of your life is dependent on modern technology? How many hours a day do you spend online or gaming? How many text messages do you send each day? Could you live without these gadgets? Are you a techno-addict?

Connecting people

The UN has reported that mobile phones are spreading quicker than any other technology. They're changing how we communicate with each other and how we live. They've become an extension of our hands and our minds, almost an essential part of us. Many British youngsters see their mobile phone as their 'best friend' and are lost without it. Have we become addicted to our mobiles?

Computer games are great fun but sometimes people spend too much of their time playing them.

34

Crazy for games

The gaming industry is a powerful and influential one. Games are an important part of many people's leisure activities and a way they relax. All over the world, children and adults alike are gripped by Nintendos, Wiis, X-boxes and other gaming devices. You can become a different character, explore other worlds and be a virtual hero. But what about what lies behind the pretty pictures, superhero actions and sense of power the player has?

SUPPLY AND DEMAND

In 2009, the UK's first **rehabilitation centre** for video game addicts opened. Each year, the centre treats 400 addicts. There are no precise numbers for the amount of addicts in the country, but it's estimated at many thousands. The key to living with technology safely is to enjoy it without letting it rule you.

Game addiction is a very real issue many people are facing today. Spending hours and hours alone in a virtual world, they find it hard to cope when they log off and have to interact with people in the normal world. This can lead to family arguments, anti-social behaviour and, in the case of young people, sleep and schoolwork being badly affected.

Game addiction can make it hard to concentrate on everyday activities such as school.

CONSUMER NATION

Are you for or against computer games?

Pros

1 They can help to improve your coordination skills.

2. They may encourage your imagination.

3. You feel a sense of achievement when you do well.

Cons

1 You spend a lot of time alone with imaginary characters rather than talking to, or playing with your real friends.

2. You find it hard to sleep so you're always tired.

3. You stay indoors and may exercise less.

CASE STUDY 3
LIVING ONLINE 24/7

Many western high-tech **IT** companies have set up **virtual sweatshops** in Eastern Europe and parts of Asia. These are where young gamers are paid to play games for other people. It may seem like the ideal job, being paid to game 24/7. It's part of a global industry worth billions of pounds. You might think that if the people are being paid a fair local salary, then what's the problem?

Staring at a screen

Picture the scene. A draughty run-down apartment block in India. In one of the flats on the fourth floor, there are rows of tables and chairs. A small kitchen has a kettle and some dirty cups. There are no pictures on the walls. On the chairs, sit a dozen young people staring at computer screens and furiously hitting keys. They don't blink, they don't talk: they just play.

Virtual sweatshops may be set up in an apartment block such as this one in India.

Some young people spend much of their free time playing computer games. Addiction to gaming can become a serious problem for virtual sweatshop workers, too.

Changeover

It's 7pm as Raj arrives at the apartment. He has come here most days for the past seven months. He's trying to pay his way through university by working the night shift. He nods to one or two of the other gamers and then takes the seat of Adil, a day-shifter.

Round the clock

Between them, 12 employees play day and night, seven days a week. An American company pays for the apartment, the computers and the workers' wages of around £70 per month. Sometimes, Raj and his colleagues are testing new games and sometimes they are paid to play on behalf of wealthy western players when they themselves are at work or asleep.

Paying for play

There are hundreds of computer games for which millions of people pay a monthly fee to keep their characters in the game. For the workers like Raj, who play on behalf of others, the games can be highly addictive. Sometimes, Raj goes in on his day off just to continue playing. His university studies are suffering and he hasn't slept properly in weeks. He doesn't talk to his family much. He hasn't got the energy or the time to find another job; he was lucky to get this one. He just can't stop playing...

Complicated problems like these aren't easy to solve, but what ideas do you have? What rules would you put in place to stop people becoming addicted to gaming, and what help would you provide for addicts?

HIGH-TECH HEALTH MATTERS

Imagine having to handle and inhale chemicals in your everyday work. What about having to look at a screen all day long? How would your eyes feel? Think about sitting at a desk for a few hours and then trying to stretch. Many stages of the technology production line involve activities that are potentially harmful to health.

Toxic technology

Did you know that behind your bright monitor is up to 4 kg of lead? The health effects of lead are well known: lead exposure causes brain damage in children and has been banned from many consumer products.

Some monitors use lead and mercury lamps; some even use poisonous arsenic. Like lead, mercury is toxic in very low doses and causes brain and kidney damage. Just 1/70th of a teaspoon of mercury is enough to contaminate 20 acres of a lake, making the fish unfit to eat. Lead dust in the air can be swallowed and passed on through breast milk.

The lead in computers can be harmful to both the factory workers and to the environment.

38

Risky business?

Millions of workers all over the world work in the technology industry, and many are exposed to harmful chemicals and practices. Indium and cadmium are two chemicals used in computers, both of which can cause kidney problems. PVC fumes can also cause breathing difficulties if used in closed spaces. The UN is campaigning for improvements to be made in the electronics and technology industries, but some damage has already been done.

Post-production problems

The problems aren't just in the manufacturing stages, though. A recent study of dust on computers in workplaces and homes found brominated flame retardants (BFRs) in every sample taken. BFRs are used in electronic products as a way of protecting against fire. BFRs may seriously affect hormonal functions which are vital for normal physical development. Alarming rates of BFRs have been found in the breast milk of women in Sweden and the USA.

SHOP TO CHANGE THE WORLD

You can play your part in helping to make the electronics industry cleaner, greener and healthier by buying products from companies that don't use harmful chemicals. Dell, Hewlett Packard, Nokia, Samsung and Sony Ericsson have made a commitment to phase out hazardous chemicals. This will make each stage of the manufacturing and disposal safer and more eco-friendly.

Ethical companies, such as this one in Shanghai, China, make sure their workers are well protected from harmful substances.

CHAPTER 5

CAMPAIGNING FOR CHANGE

There are many influential organisations and pressure groups who are making a difference to the way the technology industry operates. They strive to make things better for workers, to avoid children being **exploited**, and to improve the environmental impact of our technology.

SUPPLY AND DEMAND

The more demand there is for a product, the more money a company will make from selling it. Pressure groups work in the same way. The more people they represent, the more a company will listen to them. If they can 'supply' voices of protest, then they can 'demand' change.

Putting on the pressure

Pressure groups work to make a difference through campaigning. They target and meet with individual companies and governments in order to do this. Sometimes, they conduct undercover investigations and shame the businesses with their findings. A business will probably change their practices if they are worried about customers going elsewhere.

40

Group power

UNICEF is a UN agency looking after children's rights. The charity
Save the Children also campaigns against child labour. Campaigns from
'Make IT Fair' have also caused some technology companies to change their
ways for the better. These and other groups have online forms called
petitions that you can sign to show your support for their causes.

Eco-awareness

Environmental pressure groups, such as Greenpeace, Friends of
the Earth and Kids for Saving Earth, campaign for (and educate
people about) better use of the Earth's resources. They are also
concerned with the level of industrial pollution created by the
technology industry. For more information, see page 47.

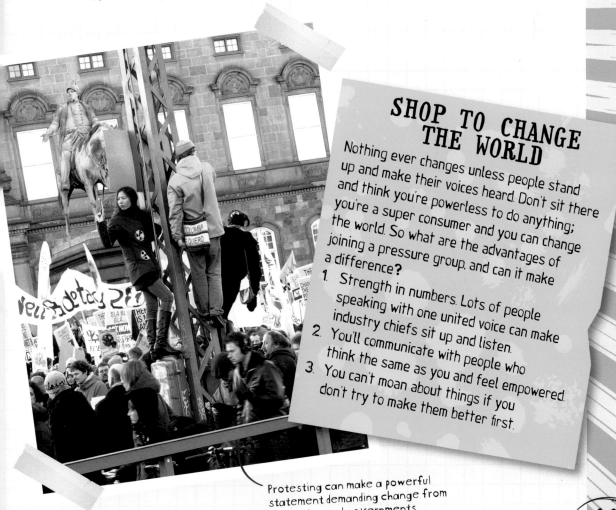

SHOP TO CHANGE THE WORLD

Nothing ever changes unless people stand
up and make their voices heard. Don't sit there
and think you're powerless to do anything;
you're a super consumer and you can change
the world. So what are the advantages of
joining a pressure group, and can it make
a difference?

1. Strength in numbers. Lots of people
   speaking with one united voice can make
   industry chiefs sit up and listen.
2. You'll communicate with people who
   think the same as you and feel empowered.
3. You can't moan about things if you
   don't try to make them better first.

Protesting can make a powerful
statement demanding change from
companies and governments.

41

SMALL STEPS TO BIG CHANGE

In towns and cities all over the world, if you look carefully, you can see small changes are happening. Some companies are making an effort to do things better and to improve things along the supply chain, for people and the planet.

SHOP TO CHANGE THE WORLD

We all like to be up to date and keep pace with our friends on the technology front, but what do you really need? It's important to understand technology and the advantages that gadgets, games and phones can give us but remember, it's about being a sensible consumer and not just having more stuff.

Cooperation

Small-scale business communities all over the world are improving their own working conditions and supply chains. In some technology factories and mineral mines, workers are starting to unite and form unions. This makes it possible for their concerns to be heard. On a larger scale, governments are starting to sign up to international legal agreements concerning human rights and environmental protection.

This modern, well-lit factory puts its workers' safety first with the correct safety clothing and equipment.

Making a change

Many technology companies are owned by shareholders, people who have bought shares in the company on the stock market. The shareholders can influence what the company does when they vote on certain decisions. The more money a shareholder has invested, the more power they have. Further along the supply chain, consumers have power, too. Finding out about how products are made, what eco-impact they have and how the workers are treated, can help us to make informed choices.

Perfect chain

It is possible to achieve a fair and eco-friendly supply chain in the technology industry, but it will take everyone involved to demand less and supply a little more in terms of time and money. For the sake of workers and the planet, companies and governments need to play by *all* the rules.

SUPPLY AND DEMAND

If your PC or phone is no longer working as fast or as well as you'd like, consider your options before you replace. You may be able to keep your handset or your tower and simply add more memory or a new battery. Remember, whatever you demand, businesses will supply – so don't let them encourage you to buy something new if you don't really need or want it.

Take a look around, find out about the product and the company...

... and make an informed choice when you buy. Encourage your family to do the same. That way, you'll really make a difference.

SHOP TO CHANGE THE WORLD

The making, selling and buying chain of any product is complicated and usually involves many different people all over the world. Everything has a cost and it's not just the one on the box of your product. We, as consumers and buyers, play a key role in this chain.

Time for change?

There are many people and organisations who are responsible for keeping things the way they are, from western companies wanting to make the most profit possible, to consumers like us wanting low prices. At some point, someone in the chain is going to suffer if things carry on in this way.

Governments of developing countries welcome the investment and the jobs that technology factories bring, but there is rarely any checking of working conditions or making sure that the workers are looked after properly. We increasingly rely on techno-gadgets to organise our lives, but it's the sweatshop workers and the environment that really pay the price.

Technology companies spend huge amounts of money marketing their products to potential buyers. Consumers can use their spending power to help create a fairer industry.

The buck stops here!

As a consumer of techno-gadgets, you have real power to change things. You are the end of the chain and if you're not happy with a product or how it's made, then companies will listen to you because they want you to buy their item. Fair trade means that shoppers can be responsible and demand fairness at all stages of the supply chain.

Today, many people buy only from companies that treat their employees and the environment well. You can avoid buying products by companies who use sweatshops, child labour, or have a poor environmental record. Our technology-based lives really shouldn't have to cost the Earth.

SUPPLY AND DEMAND

There are many campaigns launched to focus attention on working conditions in the electronics industry in developing countries. 'Clean up your computer' is run by a charity demanding that sweatshop workers in the technology industry are treated according to international working standards.

Enjoy technology but don't let it rule your life!

SHOP TO CHANGE THE WORLD

You could join a campaign group working to change conditions for technology factory workers for the better. You could also campaign for a reduction in toxic emissions. There are many online campaigns and lots of information out there. See page 47 for more details.

45

GLOSSARY

assembly   putting different pieces together to make one product

consumer   a person who buys or consumes

desalination plants   factories where seawater is changed to freshwater

developed world   industrialised countries

disability benefit   government money for disabled people who can't work

ethical shopping   buying products from companies that have a good supply chain and fair conditions for workers

exploited   taken advantage of

fair trade   fairly sharing profits along the supply chain

fossil fuels   fuels, such as coal, oil and natural gas, that form from the remains of ancient plants and animals

greenhouse gas   a gas that contributes to global warming, such as carbon dioxide and methane

human rights   the safety, security and education that every person on Earth is entitled to

landfill   rubbish tips

manufacturing costs   what it costs to make any product

maternity pay   a salary paid to women when they take time off work to have a baby

migrant workers   people who travel around seeking work

outlawed   something that is banned, or illegal

outsourcing   buying labour or materials from elsewhere, usually because it is cheaper

petitions   signed written requests for change

poverty   not having enough money for basic needs such as food, clothes or housing

pressure groups   campaign groups who put pressure on governments or companies to change

rehabilitation centre   a place where games addicts can go to receive medical help

solvents   substances that dissolve other substances to form a solution

supply chain   all the people and materials that go into making and distributing a product

sweatshops   factories with poor working conditions and low pay

toxic   poisonous

UN   stands for the United Nations, an international organisation founded in 1945 to promote peace, security and economic development

virtual sweatshops   places of work with conditions like a factory sweatshop

water courses   groundwater

FOR MORE INFORMATION

Books

Explore: Fair Trade by Jillian Powell, Wayland 2012

Hot Topics: Fair Trade by Jilly Hunt, Raintree 2012

Boys Without Names by Kashmira Sheth, HarperCollins 2011

Natural Resources by Amy Bauman, TickTock 2008

Websites

For UK firms that collect, repair and recycle old electronic equipment, visit:
www.ecocomputersystems.org.uk

If you're interested in joining a pressure group or finding out more about being a super consumer, check out the following websites:

www.dosomething.org
This is a great website for teenagers to get involved in issues you care about.

www.sweatfree.org/shopping
Explore this website and see what this charity is doing to assist sweatshop workers around the world.

www.betterworldshopper.org
This website rates companies on thier social and environmental responsibility.

www.greenpeace.org
Check out this website and find out about environmental issues and what you can do to make a difference.

www.kidsforsavingearth.org
This website is all about how you can help to protect our planet.

INDEX